BITE INTO
Bloodsuckers

by KARI-LYNN WINTERS
and ISHTA MERCURIO

Fitzhenry & Whiteside

DEDICATION

For Meredith Tutching, who, to my knowledge, has never been a sucker or a vampire.

——KARI-LYNN WINTERS

This book is dedicated to the mosquito, one of the toughest and most adaptable creatures on Earth.

——ISHTA MERCURIO

ACKNOWLEDGMENTS

Jonah for his ongoing support and for his line edits. Solange and Cheryl for their eagle eyes and for keeping us on our toes. Ishta, for being the dedicated and awesome researcher/writer that she is.

——KARI-LYNN WINTERS

The Wentworth clan: Walker, Asher, and Carter, for their creative ideas, patience, guinea piggery, and a steady stream of snacks and coffee. The lovely experts at the Royal Ontario Museum, for being so kind in lending their expertise: Antonia Guidotti, entomologist; Margaret Zur, Ichthyologist; and finally Henry Choong and Maureen Zubowski, invertebrate zoologists. Kari-Lynn Winters, for inviting me to join her on this adventure. Solange Messier, for getting us off to an amazing start.

——ISHTA MERCURIO

Published in Canada by Fitzhenry & Whiteside Limited,
195 Allstate Parkway, Markham, ON   L3R 4T8

Published in the United States by
Fitzhenry & Whiteside Limited, 311 Washington Street, Brighton, MA 02135

Canada Council   Conseil des arts
for the Arts   du Canada

ONTARIO ARTS COUNCIL
CONSEIL DES ARTS DE L'ONTARIO
an Ontario government agency
un organisme du gouvernement de l'Ontario

Fitzhenry & Whiteside acknowledges with thanks the Canada Council for the Arts, and the Ontario Arts Council for their support of our publishing program. We acknowledge the financial support of the Government of Canada through the Canada Book Fund (CBF) for our publishing activities.

Cover and interior design by Tanya Montini
Proudly printed in Canada by Advanced Printing

Library and Archives Canada Cataloguing in Publication
Title: Glow-in-the-dark creatures / by Natalie Hyde.
Names: Hyde, Natalie, 1963- author. Description: Previously published: Markham, Ontario: Fitzhenry & Whiteside, 2014. | Includes bibliographical references and index.
Identifiers: Canadiana 20200218026 | ISBN 9781554555420 (softcover)
Classification: LCC QH641 .H93 2020 | DDC j572/.4358—dc23

Publisher Cataloging-in-Publication Data (U.S.)
Names: Hyde, Natalie, 1963-, author.
Title: Glow in the Dark Creatures / by Natalie Hyde.
Description: Markham, Ontario : Fitzhenry & Whiteside, 2020. | Originally published in hardcover 2014. | Includes bibliography and index. | Summary: "Glow-in-the-dark creatures possess one of the most amazing abilities in our world. Using only chemicals in their bodies, they can create bioluminescence, or 'living light'. Glow-in-the-dark creatures use their light displays to hide from enemies, to cry for help, to warn of danger or to find a mate. From fireflies and glowworms to flashlight fish and velvet belly lantern sharks, the diversity and number of creatures who are bioluminescent have surprised scientists" -- Provided by publisher.
 Identifiers: ISBN 978-1-55455-330-3 (hc.) 978-1-55455-542-0 (pbk.)
 Subjects: LCSH Animals – Adaptation – Juvenile literature. | Bioluminescence – Juvenile literature. | BISAC: JUVENILE NONFICTION / Animals / General.
Classification: LCC QH641.H93 |DDC 572.4358 – dc23

CONTENTS

I Vant to Suck Your Blood!

OUT FOR BLOOD

Most people hear the word "vampire" and think of shady characters with capes and pointed teeth. Some famous fictional vampires include The Count from *Sesame Street*, Count Dracula, and Draculaura from *Monster High*. These mythical characters are said to be nocturnal, sleeping in coffins all day and coming out at night to hunt for necks to bite. Sunlight turns them to ash. They have pale skin and hate garlic. But that's all pretend...right?

Yes and no. Bloodsucking vampires really do exist, but not in the ways stories portray them—for one thing, they aren't people! Most bloodsuckers are **parasites** that feed on their **hosts'** blood in order to survive. These bloodthirsty creatures come in many shapes and sizes. Whether they are worm-like leeches, six-legged flying insects, eight-legged arachnids, birds, fish, or small **mammals**, they have one thing in common: they practise bloodsucking, which is also known as hematophagy (HEE-muh-TAW-fuh-jee). They thrive on the blood of mammals, birds, reptiles, and amphibians. When these vampire critters latch on, their bites can range from annoying to deadly, depending on the type of parasite, the host's physical reaction to the bite, and the diseases these parasites carry.

WHAT IS BLOOD?

Blood is essential for all **vertebrates** to live. It is made up of red blood cells that carry oxygen to the brain and other parts of the body, white blood cells that fight disease, plasma,

Some parasites, like tapeworms, are endoparasites, which means that they live inside their hosts. Other parasites, called ectoparasites, live on the outside of their hosts. They often pierce or bore holes in their hosts' skin in order to access the protein-rich blood.

and water. Blood also transports nutrients throughout the body and carries liquid waste to the kidneys, which then eliminate the waste from the body. Blood is important; without it, humans and other vertebrates would die.

BLOOD FOR SURVIVAL

Humans need blood in their bodies to live, but they can't survive on a blood diet like some bloodsucking creatures do. In fact, people rarely consume blood for many reasons. It doesn't smell good, it's not as easy to obtain as fruits and vegetables, and it doesn't taste very good because it is very salty. Vampire creatures, on the other hand, have special digestive systems that help them absorb and digest blood's ingredients, including the salt and minerals. Many bloodsuckers survive on blood alone. For instance, bed bugs, one type of vampire creature, feed solely on the blood of mammals and birds for their nourishment. Others, like mosquitoes, may feast on plant nectar for nourishment. Only female mosquitoes drink blood, and they do it only to get the protein they need to produce eggs. Male mosquitoes never take in a bloody meal.

AT STAKE

There are many reasons why humans cannot survive by drinking blood. One of them is that although people need salt—a vital mineral—in their diets, too much salt can be dangerous. If a person drank blood every day, he or she would likely have higher **blood pressure**, and be at an increased risk for kidney disease, heart attacks, and bleeding in the brain (called a stroke). More importantly, many serious diseases are transmitted through bodily fluids, such as blood. Moreover, in chapter 10 we talk about how bloodsuckers can be vectors for diseases like malaria and Lyme disease. If people drink raw blood, they put themselves at a greater risk for contracting diseases.

Blood transports oxygen, nutrients, and liquid waste to where it needs to go inside the body.

Blood Brothers

Madrilenial butterflies. African zimbs.
Deer ticks. Dog ticks.
Get off my limbs!

The varroa mite or vampire finch.
Lampreys. Assassin bugs.
Bite, drink, pinch!

Thousands of mosquitoes sip blood—so sweet!
Deer flies. Horseflies.
Oh, spray me with DEET!

The bloodsucking bed bug—what a parasite!
This fierce, piercing pest
bites its victims at night.

Freshwater leech. I'm not your steak!
That's the last time
I swim in your lake.

Thinking of lice makes me twitch.
Head louse. Body louse.
Scritch, scratch, itch.

Vampire bat. Chicken flea.
Oxpecker. Kissing bug.
Get off of me!

CHAPTER 2

Warm-Blooded Slurpers

GOT (WARM) BLOOD?

Mammals are warm-blooded creatures. This means that, unlike reptiles that warm up by lying in the sun, mammals have to generate body heat in order to survive. That takes a lot of energy! In fact, most of the food that mammals eat is converted into energy to stay warm. The bigger the body, the more energy it requires to stay warm. The more energy needed to stay warm, the more a creature has to eat. This is one of the reasons that mammals are usually not blood drinkers—fresh blood is much harder to come by than most other food sources.

FLESH AND BLOOD

We've said that humans do not survive solely on blood, but believe it or not, meat-eaters consume some blood in their diets. In fact, any person who eats red meat has also eaten blood. Meat is actually the muscles of a vertebrate. Red meat (like beef and the dark meat from a turkey) is red because of the extra blood that was pumped to it to supply the muscle with oxygen while the animal was alive. That's why an undercooked steak leaks pinkish or red juices when it is cut: the redder the juices, the less cooked (or rarer) the steak is. It's also why it is important to cook meat thoroughly, because sufficient heat kills viruses and bacteria that are carried through the blood of an infected creature.

BLOOD FEASTS

In some countries, blood is the main ingredient in certain foods. In the United Kingdom, blood sausage, also known as black pudding, is made by taking the strained blood of a pig or cow and combining it with a filler, like oats, rice, or barley. The mixture is then stuffed into a sausage casing and cooked. Tibetans have many uses for yak blood, including using it as an ingredient in blood sausage and in bread. They may also boil or fry congealed yak blood. In some Asian countries, like China, congealed blood from pigs and poultry is known as "blood tofu" and is deep fried and eaten. And in Finland, blood pancakes are made with equal parts pig blood, milk, and rye flour, and are served with lingonberry jam.

Anyone who has eaten red meat before has also eaten blood.

Additionally, some cultures drink raw blood as a part of their diets. The Maasai, in Kenya, mix the blood of cattle with milk and drink it on special occasions, such as after giving birth or when sick. This is because their culture was traditionally dependent on livestock, such as cattle and goats, as both a primary source of food and a valuable item for trade. Since blood contains extra protein and minerals (such as **iron**), the Maasai believe that drinking it is a good way to boost the immune system and replace depleted stores of iron. However, according to The Maasai Association, in recent years the Maasai have experienced a change in their way of life. Climate change has led to more drought in their region, which makes raising livestock difficult. As they cultivate more crops and raise fewer livestock, their source of blood for drinking has shrunk, and they have added less blood to their diet.

> Newborn vampire bats don't drink blood! They drink only their mother's milk for the first three months of their lives.

VAMPIRE BATS

Vampire bats are the only mammals that feed solely on blood. Because finding a source for a good blood meal can be challenging, and because the act of drinking blood is hard work for vampire bats, they don't have a lot of energy left over for growing. Compared to many of their fruit-eating cousins, vampire bats are quite small. Their bodies range from 7 to 9 centimetres (about 3 to 3.5 inches) long, and they weigh approximately 28 grams (2 ounces).

Vampire bats feed mostly on sleeping livestock: pigs, horses, goats, cows, and sometimes birds. While humans are definitely not their primary food source, there have been instances where livestock has become so scarce that vampire bats have resorted to biting humans. A vampire bat uses its sense of sound (echolocation) and its limited sight to locate its host. Then it lands on the ground nearby and hops over to its intended victim. A heat sensor on its nose tells it where the animal's warm blood is flowing closest to the skin. It carefully crawls to the best spot, then uses its teeth to nip away any hairs that are covering the skin. Typically, a vampire bat makes a small cut, ranging from three to five millimetres (0.1 to 0.2 inches), from which a very small amount of blood will ooze. It laps the blood, using its tongue. A groove running

Vampire bats are the only mammals that feed solely on blood.

along the underside of its tongue expands and contracts with the lapping motion, carrying the blood up into its mouth. Normally a cut that small would only leak a drop or two of blood before the blood begins to clot, but vampire bats have a special **anticoagulant** (ANT-eye-co-AG-you-lant) in their saliva that stops clotting from occurring. The blood will continue to flow, making it possible for not only one vampire bat to obtain a full meal, but for several bats in a row to feed from the same wound.

After about thirty minutes of feeding, a vampire bat is nice and full. Sometimes, a blood meal will double a bat's body weight! This makes it hard to take off and fly away. Fortunately, vampire bats only need the most nutritious part of blood, which is the red and white blood cells. Vampire bats have a specialized stomach that can absorb the less nutritious plasma part of blood quickly and send it to their kidneys. The red and white blood cells remain in the stomach for digestion, while the diluted plasma gets peed out about two minutes after feeding. This lightens the load and makes it easier to take flight.

SHARING IN THE BLOOD BATH

Vampire bats do not kill their victims. First, even a group of four or five bats could never drink enough blood at one time to drain a creature as large as a pig or a cow. Second, by not killing their victims, bats can share the blood and even return to the same host to feed repeatedly over a period of weeks. If an animal dies because of a bat bite, it is because the bat has transmitted a disease, like rabies, to the animal through the bite.

In addition to sharing hosts, female bats bond with each other by grooming each other. Once finished, the groomed bat vomits up part of her blood meal to share with the grooming bat as a thank-you gift. Mother bats bond with their young in a similar way, feeding them regurgitated blood during the fourth and fifth months of a young bat's life.

CHAPTER 3

Pecking Orders

VAMPIRE FINCHES

Ground finches in the Galapagos Islands usually eat seeds. But one type of ground finch, the vampire finch, has a longer, sharper beak than most other birds of its kind. This beak is useful for sipping nectar from cactus flowers and cracking open the eggs of seabirds to eat the insides. But it is the other use of its beak that gives the vampire finch its name. These small black male or brownish-streaked female vampires occasionally use their sharp beaks to peck at the base of a large seabird's tail and wing feathers—until they draw blood. Once the skin is pierced, the finches gather in groups around the seabird to lap up its blood. For the adult seabird that is victimized, these little freeloaders can be quite annoying. For the seabird's young (both chicks and unhatched), the pecks from the sharp-beaked finches can be deadly.

Scientists are still studying vampire finches to figure out how they came to drink blood. The most popular theory is that they originally had a symbiotic relationship with a seabird called the red-footed booby: this means that they did something that benefitted the boobies, and the boobies did something that benefitted them. In this case, the finches ate the ticks and black flies that lived in the boobies' feathers and fed on the boobies' blood. This benefitted both the finches, who had a reliable food source, and the seabirds, who had fewer annoying bugs biting them!

It is believed that eating blood-drinking insects gave the finches a taste for blood. The insects would have been full of blood, and therefore would have tasted like blood. While pecking at these pests, the birds may have opened up wounds on the seabirds' bodies and then begun to feed from the bloody wounds. Australian filmmaker David Parer even filmed finches drinking the blood seeping from wounds on his feet and hands when he held very still.

The vampire finch uses its long, sharp beak to sip nectar, but it also uses it to peck at skin and draw blood.

Hood mockingbirds from the Galapagos Islands feed on seabird parasites (e.g., ticks), sometimes lapping up the blood of wounded seabirds.

BIRDS THAT WANT BLOOD

In Sub-Saharan Africa, red-billed oxpeckers perch on the backs, heads, and legs of large mammals, such as giraffes and rhinoceroses. They hop along the larger animals' bodies, eating the ticks and pesky insects that can be found there, so they have fewer pests to worry about. They also help keep them clean by slurping up any excess mucus and earwax!

But is that really what's going on? In 2004, **biologist** Alan McElligott and his colleagues studied red-billed oxpeckers and African black rhinoceroses in captivity, and what they found surprised them. They expected to see the oxpeckers pecking at wounds occasionally, but the oxpeckers spent much less time eating ticks and bugs than they spent drinking blood from their large hosts. In fact, they seemed to ignore ticks that were sitting right out in the open on the rhinoceroses' backs in favour of pecking and lapping at bloody wounds.

What's more, these birds, like vampire finches, were seen for the first time creating new wounds in the rhinoceroses' hides in order to lap up their blood. They did this by first picking at loose skin with their beaks, pulling at it until a piece of it came off, and then pecking at the wound, which enlarged the hole, increased blood flow, and created more loose skin to pull off. Those birds wanted blood!

Red-billed oxpeckers hunt for ticks on the bodies of larger animals, such as impalas, but also peck at wounds and lap up blood.

11

It is said that some people get bitten more often by mosquitoes because they smell sweeter. While this isn't necessarily the case, it is true that mosquitoes prefer a certain balance of CO_2, octenol, and other **hormones**. If your sweat has the right amounts of each chemical, then you will be at the top of the mosquito menu.

Fliers and Buzzers

WHO'S THAT BUZZING IN MY EAR?

Ah, the sounds of summer: the rumble of a lawnmower, the hissing of a garden sprinkler, the high-pitched whine of…a mosquito right behind your ear! No matter where you live in the world, you have probably met a mosquito (or ten) in your lifetime. With over 3,500 identified species, these buzzing pests are among the most common bloodsucking insects in the world. But they don't all suck blood—in fact, their primary source of food is sugar from plant nectar. Female mosquitoes, however, need both sugar for energy and blood protein for egg production, and it's these little ladies who you hear buzzing in your ear.

Mosquitoes identify their hosts by sensing a combination of chemicals including **carbon dioxide** (CO_2), lactic acid, and octenol, which is a hormone humans produce that smells a lot like mushrooms. When a female mosquito identifies a possible host, she gently prods the host's skin with her **proboscis** for a few seconds before piercing the skin with her highly specialized mouthparts. The visible part of a female mosquito's proboscis is actually a sheath that covers and protects her mouthparts, which include pointed mandibles and toothed maxillae (mak-SILL-ee) for piercing the skin. There are also two tubes: one for pumping her saliva into the host and one for drawing blood. Mosquito saliva includes not only an anticoagulant, but also a chemical that opens up the host's blood vessels to increase blood flow, and other chemicals that temporarily inhibit the host's **immune system**. This information is important for understanding mosquitoes' role in spreading diseases among humans.

Only female mosquitoes suck blood.

NOT HORSING AROUND

Adult horseflies, sometimes called zimbs or clegs, are large flies that typically survive on nectar and pollen. However, in order to reproduce, female horseflies need protein. Where do they find this protein? In blood, of course!

These vampires slash through their hosts' fur and skin using sharp, blade-like mouthparts. Then they lap the flowing blood with a sponge-like organ called a **labella**. Female horseflies can lap blood in this way for up to six hours!

Farmers use fly traps and sprays to rid their fields and stables of horseflies. This is because female horseflies, when on the hunt for blood, become a nuisance to livestock and ultimately to the farmers themselves. They have been known to swarm cattle to such an extent that the cattle feel threatened and produce less milk. Also, these irritating pests are sometimes the cause of injuries, both from the bite wounds themselves and from the accidents caused when the cattle or horses try to escape.

Like the mosquito, only the female horseflies drink blood.

BATTLE OF THE BLOODSUCKERS

Similarities:

Horseflies have several things in common with mosquitoes. First, horseflies and mosquitoes are both flies. In fact, the name mosquito, when translated from Spanish, means "little fly." They both belong in the order *Diptera*, meaning insects with two wings. Second, the main food source for both horseflies and mosquitoes is plant nectar, and in both species only the females drink blood. As mentioned before, blood contains protein, which is needed for egg production. Third, both horseflies and mosquitoes can be annoying, especially for livestock and humans, and they both have the potential to carry and spread diseases. Fourth, both female horseflies and mosquitoes can detect movement, chemicals and **hormones**, and heat; they use all three of these abilities to find their hosts.

Differences:

However, horseflies and mosquitoes are unique, too. While female horseflies use their knife-like mandibles to rip apart

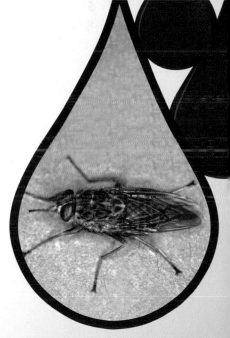

Zebras, which live in Africa and are part of the same family as horses, are pestered by tsetse flies. But scientists have discovered that tsetse flies do not like stripes. This may be why zebras with greater striping are bitten less often.

TOP: Horseflies use their mandibles to tear flesh. BOTTOM: Mosquitoes, however, use their hypostomes to pierce skin.

Taste-sensitive receptors can be found on the deer fly's body and feet.

flesh, leaving a bloody wound, female mosquitoes have strong needle-like mouthparts called hypostomes (HI-puh-stohms) that pierce through skin or hide. Once they have pierced the skin, they pump in their saliva filled with anticoagulants, which make the blood flow, and **enzymes** (ENZ-eyemz), which numb the skin. When the mosquito is finished or disturbed, she will fly away. Unlike horsefly bites, which are painful, a mosquito bite feels itchy because the immune system is trying to fight off the saliva.

Aside from having different mouthparts and leaving different wounds, horseflies and mosquitoes are distinct in other ways, too. For example, while horseflies prefer the daytime, mosquitoes are most active before sunrise and after sundown. This may be why, unlike mosquitoes, horseflies are rarely found in barns or shady places like forests.

SENSING A BLOOD BUFFET

Deer flies, also known as stouts, can see, smell, hear, touch, and taste. Female deer flies use all of these senses when searching for blood.

Smelling:

Covered in microscopic receptors, the antennae allow the deer fly to detect humidity, but more importantly, to smell odours and carbon dioxide. These antennae help them zone in on their bloody meals.

Hearing:

Like humans, deer flies have eardrums that sense sound waves in their environments. But unlike human ears, the ears of deer flies are located near their front legs. Hearing movements helps them drop in on their prey.

Touching:

Small hairs on the deer fly let it know it has landed on its meal. Attached to small nerves just under the deer fly's skin, these hairs can also detect air movements, as well as their flying orientation (i.e., which direction is up or down).

Tasting:

Imagine using your body or your feet to taste. Taste-sensitive receptors can be found on the deer fly's body and feet. Most insects can taste bitter, sweet, sour, and salty flavours.

Seeing:

The first thing you may notice about a deer fly's head is its two brightly coloured compound eyes. These big eyes, with their multiple honeycomb-like lenses, enable this stalker to see in different directions at the same time! Deer flies are especially attracted to dark colours and to movement.

SALTY SIPS

Vampire moths, called calyptra (cuh-LIP-truh) moths, were originally thought to be vegetarians—only feeding on fruit. Recently however, scientists discovered that when male moths were offered a cut finger, they voluntarily took a sip of blood. Experts believe that the moths might be in search of the salt in the blood, which they pass on to the female moths during mating to help develop stronger **larvae**.

Much like mosquitoes, vampire moths use their pointed proboscises to pierce the skin of humans or other vertebrates. These moths then drink the blood, sometimes until their small stomachs are full. Unlike mosquitoes though, whose females are responsible for any annoying bites, male moths are the bloodsuckers. The wounds from a male vampire's proboscis may hurt more than the puncture of a female mosquito.

BEAUTIFUL BLOODERFLIES

He looks harmless, and even handsome, as he flutters down. Yet, the Spanish madrilenial butterfly has a darker side. This seemingly innocent insect has a specialized diet: not only does he sip nectar, but he also drinks blood. Once he locates and lands on his meal, he uses his tube-like proboscis to sip blood until he is full.

While most bloodsuckers prefer to drink from living organisms, the madrilenial butterfly craves the blood of dead animals, like cattle and reptiles. Some theories suggest these male butterflies might be seeking out minerals, such as salt (sodium) or amino acids. It is believed that these liquid nutrients can then be passed to the female butterfly during mating, improving the couple's eggs and ensuring better reproductive success. The blood, in this way, can be seen as a sort of wedding gift!

TOP: Deer flies have large compound eyes which allow them to see in different directions at the same time.
BOTTOM: While female mosquitoes and horseflies drink blood, only male vampire moths and madrilennial butterflies are bloodsuckers.

CHAPTER 5

Ticks breathe very, very slowly. They only need to take between three and fifteen breaths per hour. That's one breath every 4 to 20 minutes!

A tick can drink up to 600 times its weight in blood

Crawlers

WHAT MAKES A TICK TICK?

Ticks, like many other bloodsuckers, need blood in order to develop and produce offspring. There are two types of ticks: soft ticks and hard ticks. When feeding, a soft female tick can blow up like a balloon! Soft ticks have two main body parts: a head with a beak (called a capitulum), which includes the mouthparts and eyes, and a leathery body, which includes the tick's eight legs. Mouthparts, including the hypostome, are located on the underside of the tick. Hard ticks have an additional body part: a protective plate (called a scutum) on their backs. Hard ticks do not become as engorged as soft ticks and are slow eaters, sometimes drinking the host's blood for a day or two.

SEVEN HABITS OF HIGHLY ANNOYING TICKS

1. Creeping around.

2. Grabbing onto you when you least expect it.

3. Stabbing you with a harpoon-like mouthpart (hypostome).

4. Clinging to your body with their mouthparts.

5. Spitting liquid (an anticoagulant) into you to keep your blood flowing.

6. Guzzling your blood until they are nearly bursting.

7. Leaving their heads inside you if you flick their bodies away.

DON'T LET THE BED BUGS BITE

Bed bugs are becoming a nuisance internationally. They have been found in homes, libraries, and even in the fanciest hotels. These vampires feed on the blood of mammals, including humans. Bed bugs are mostly nocturnal, which means that they sleep during the day and are active at night. They feed while their hosts sleep. They prefer exposed skin, such as their host's neck, arms, and legs.

A bed bug's compound eyes allow it to see movement. Its two antennae also help it to search out its prey's scent and breath. Like other bloodsuckers, these pests pierce the skin of their prey with their beak-like mouth parts. However, because their bites are painless, victims sometimes don't even realize they were bitten until the morning. If you have a bed bug infestation, it is common to become a bed bug's night-time meal and then to wake up to a bunch of itchy, red bumps!

Bed bugs were common in North America until the early-to-mid 20th century, when they were almost wiped out by bug-killing chemicals called pesticides. But thanks to an increase in international travel, increased pesticide resistance in bed bugs, and pesticide bans in the late 20th century, they're baaaa-ack!

An adult bed bug is about the size of a sesame seed. But don't let its small size fool you. It has a large appetite for blood. A single bed bug molts, meaning it sheds its skin, five times before it is fully grown, and it has to feed before each molt. These sneaky parasites like to live in cozy places, like on a mattress edge or in your pillow. At night, they come out. They detect and use various cues (e.g., movement, carbon dioxide levels, hormones, heat) to find their blood meals.

Between 20% and 25% of people don't react to bed bug bites. That's between one-fifth and one-quarter of the population. You could be living with bed bugs and never know!

THE KISS OF DEATH

Imagine waking up and looking in the mirror to find your mouth surrounded by itchy red welts. What happened? Well, if you live in the southwestern United States, Central America, or South America, you just might have been paid a visit by a kissing bug.

Kissing bugs are triatomines—a sub-family of cone-nosed insects with dark brown-to-black oval-shaped bodies that

Bed Bug Anatomy

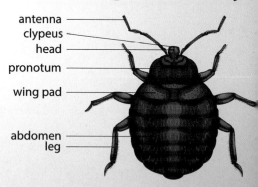

antenna
clypeus
head
pronotum

wing pad

abdomen
leg

A kissing bug bites most commonly around its victim's mouth, which is how it got its name.

The masked hunter disguises itself as a tiny dust ball and feeds on other insects.

have stripes on the sides. All 138 identified species drink blood, and most drink the blood of vertebrates, while a few drink the blood of other insects. They usually live in their hosts' "nests". The five species of kissing bug that typically bite humans live in the cracks and thatched roofs of dwellings in countries like Brazil, Chile, and Peru. These nocturnal insects drop down from the ceiling onto their victims, extend their proboscises, and pierce the hosts' skin with their mouthparts.

Kissing bugs will bite a human anywhere on the body, but the most common location of these bites is on the face, especially around the mouth. Unfortunately, mild itchiness around the wounds is not the only result of a kissing-bug bite. Sometimes, a kissing bug is carrying a tiny parasite that causes Chagas disease, a disease that can cause multiple organ failure decades later. In recent years, climate change has been pushing kissing bugs farther north. Deforestation in the Amazon and increased local populations have driven more and more kissing bugs out of the wild and into people's homes. If you live in an area where kissing bugs thrive and you discover kissing bugs living in your home, it is best to hire an exterminator to get rid of them as quickly as possible.

BLOODSUCKING THE BLOODSUCKERS

The masked hunter (Reduvius personatus), one type of assassin bug, is a vampire critter that doesn't drink the blood of humans or other mammals. Instead, it feeds on the blood of other insects, including bloodsuckers like bed bugs. It gets its name "the masked hunter" because its nymphs have tiny hairs all over their bodies that pick up bits of dust until the whole body is covered. It looks like a tiny walking dust ball! This camouflage allows it to sneak up on its prey without being noticed. Masked hunters are common in southern parts of Canada. They can be found in attics, basements, and other indoor places where their prey tend to breed. As adults, they look a lot like their cousin the kissing bug, but are completely black. If you see one in your house, don't try to catch it, because it might get scared and pierce you in defence. Besides, there's no need to get rid of it—this guy is on your side!

MIGHTY MITE

Mites are some of the most successful vampire critters around. These microscopic eight-legged creatures live in a wide variety of **habitats**—in soil, in water, on plants, and on all sorts of animals including small mammals, humans, and insects. Different species can survive on wildly different diets, too. Of over 48,000 identified species, hundreds of them are known to be associated with bees alone. One species in particular, *Varroa destructor*, attaches itself to the outside of a honey bee larva and drinks the bee's blood, passing on viruses that lead to deformed wings and leaving open wounds through which other infections can pass into the bee. In less than two weeks, an infestation of the varroa mite in a bee colony can become so severe that the entire colony will die.

Other species of mites infest birds. Bird mites live in the nests of their hosts, taking blood meals from the birds and laying eggs on the hosts' skin and in their feathers. They multiply so quickly that there can be tens of thousands of mites living in a nest while young birds are being reared. If there are too many mites in one nest, or if the baby birds grow up and leave the nest, the mites will migrate in one large group to a new nest. It is during this migration period that bird mites may enter the homes of humans. While these mites prefer birds, they won't hesitate to bite humans if they find their way into a house.

There are over 48,000 identified species of mites.

LOUSY LICE

Many schools have head-lice checks. Head lice are famous for being difficult to eliminate. Once lice move in, the only option you have is to go through a thorough de-lousing ritual. Special shampoos can be used to kill the lice and eggs. Combing with a special comb also helps to get rid of all the eggs, and if you want to be extra-safe, washing all clothes, sheets, towels, and curtains in super-hot water can kill any remaining lice. Even one remaining louse can lay enough eggs on your hair to create an infestation of many lice in a matter of days.

Many people believe that the cleanest hair is the most appealing to a mommy louse, but according to the American Academy of Dermatology, lice do not distinguish between clean hair and dirty hair. Lice especially love bushy hair, because they can burrow right down under the hair and hide close to the scalp, where it is nice and warm. However, hair in dreadlocks or braids is less appealing for lice, because tying hair back in this way makes it difficult for them to get down through the hair to the scalp. This doesn't mean that people with dreadlocks or braids never get lice; they do! It's just less likely. And if someone with dreadlocks does get lice, it's hard to get rid of the lice without cutting the dreadlocks off.

Nice for Lice:
DOES YOUR HAIR MEASURE UP?

TRUE or FALSE?

1. People who do not wash their hair are more likely to have lice.

2. Wearing your hair pulled back in braids is a good way to prevent lice.

3. People with dreadlocks are more likely to have lice.

4. There are special shampoos that can be purchased to kill lice.

5. Many schools conduct regular lice checks.

Answers: 1) False 2) True 3) False 4) True 5) True

CHAPTER 6

Swimmers

LEECHING BENEATH YOUR SKIN

Not all leeches drink blood, but many species do feed
on the blood of vertebrates. Typically lean and thin,
these carnivorous segmented worms (annelids)
can become very round when engorged with
blood. Leeches detect their prey using their eyes
and special sensory cells with bristles. Using these
motion-sensitive sensory cells, freshwater leeches
can distinguish between common water movements,
like waves, and disrupted water movements, like the
splashing of their hosts. They can also detect moving
shadows and sense changes in temperature. Some, like
the medicinal leech (*Hirudo medicinalis*), have semi-circular,
blade-like jaws. They feed by attaching their sucker-like mouths
to their hosts and pressing these jaws against their host's body.
They then secrete an anticoagulant into their host, along with
an anaesthetic (AN-iss-THEHT-ick) so that their host will
not feel the pain of the bite. If the leech is pulled off the host
before it is finished feeding, the wound may continue to bleed
for several minutes. However, unlike ticks, leeches do not leave
their heads or any other body parts inside the host if pulled
off during a feast.

To get a leech off of a person before it is finished feasting,
gently but firmly slide your finger toward the wound. Then
flick the leech away so that it doesn't reattach itself. It is not
recommended to burn the leech or to dose the area with
insect repellent or salt, as this might cause the leech to vomit
into the wound, causing infection.

Some freshwater leeches can live for a year without eating a meal.

SUCKERED!

Lampreys are eel-like creatures recognizable by their large
eyes, the external nostril on the top of their heads, the seven
gill slits on each side of their heads, and especially their
unique mouths. Some lampreys are harmless, while others
drink blood. Parasitic lampreys, the ones that drink blood,
almost always feed on fish; they rarely attack humans.

Using the teeth in its suction mouth, the lamprey latches
onto its host. Then using its tongue, which is covered in rasp-

like teeth—up to 125 of them—it scrapes the fish's skin until it is raw and open. Next this vampire injects an anticoagulant into its victim. Finally the sucking begins. A lamprey can drink for four to five hours, but in some cases, they can remain attached to their host for several days!

Lampreys live in both coastal and fresh bodies of water. Since lampreys are native to the Atlantic Ocean, the sea lamprey is an invasive species in the Great Lakes. This pest's feeding habits have had devastating effects on freshwater ecosystems and have caused millions of dollars of damage to the fishing industry.

Invasive species: a non-native species which is carried to a new habitat and thrives due to a lack of natural predators, often resulting in the decline of native species.

The Cooper's nutmeg can sense chemicals in it's prey's mucus from 24 metres (79 feet) away. That's the length of a school basketball court!

CATCHING (AND DRAINING) SOME RAYS

The Cooper's nutmeg (*Cancellaria cooperii*), sometimes called the torpedo snail, is a sea snail that lives in the Pacific Ocean off the coasts of California and Mexico. It is prized by divers for its beautiful shell, which is 5 to 8 centimetres (2 to 3 inches) long. Very little is known about this beautiful creature, but in 1997, a group of scuba-diving scientists discovered that for the *Torpedo californica*, an electric ray living in the same waters, the beautiful Cooper's nutmeg is a dreaded sight.

The Cooper's nutmeg lies very still, half-buried in the sand at the sea floor, until its prey comes within smelling distance. As soon as a ray is detected, the Cooper's nutmeg scoots at a rate of 14 centimetres (5.5 inches) a minute towards the ray. That may seem slow, but it's faster than an earthworm! Once the snail reaches its host, it probes it with its tentacles and 10-centimetre (4-inch) long proboscis, searching for the ray's soft belly.

The proboscis is tipped with razor-sharp teeth called radula, which the snail uses to snip a hole in the ray's unprotected skin. As the ray lies half-buried in the sand on the ocean floor, the sea snail inserts its proboscis into the wound and sucks the ray's blood for up to 40 minutes at a time, then returns to its hiding place in the sand to digest its meal.

This snail has also been observed inserting its proboscis into previous wounds and into rays' gill holes and mouths!

PALE AROUND THE GILLS

The candiru (can-DEE-roo) is a small, thin catfish that lives in the upper Amazon River and Orinoco River basins in South America. It is transparent and tiny—only 2.5 to 5 centimetres (1 to 2 inches) long—and these qualities enable it to escape detection by larger fish and to feed more easily.

Not much is known about the candiru. No one is sure how it finds its prey. Some scientists believe that it follows the trail of stinky ammonia that larger fish leave as they pee in the water. However, an experiment in which ammonia was dripped through a tank filled with candirus failed to prove that theory. Other scientists believe that candirus use the black eyes perched on top of their heads to see their prey, but since they live in muddy waters, visibility is poor, even for a creature with good eyesight. How this bloodsucker finds its victims remains a mystery.

What is not a mystery, however, is how it feeds. It swims into the gill cavities of larger fish and uses spikes on the edges of its own gill covers to latch onto the fleshy insides of its host's gills. It uses tiny teeth to slice into an artery. Its host's blood flows out of the cut and straight into the candiru's mouth. There is no need to suck or lap. When it is full, the candiru turns around and swims out of its host to burrow into the sandy bottom of the riverbed to digest its blood meal. It will stay there, hidden, until it is time to feed again.

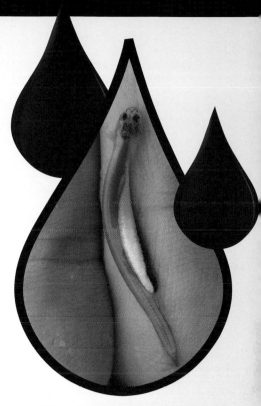

There has only been one documented case of a candiru feasting on a human.

CHAPTER 7

NORTH AMERICA
Mosquitoes
Bed bugs
Leeches
Lampreys
Biting midges
Ticks
Sand flies
Black flies
Horseflies
Deer flies
Lice
Vampire bats
(Mexican tropics)

Where Bloodsuckers Live and Bleed

Vampire creatures live on every continent. This map shows some bloodsuckers and where they live.

SOUTH AMERICA
Ticks
Kissing bugs
Sand flies
Fleas
Lice
Vampire bats
Candiru

EUROPE
Horse flies
Vampire moths
Madrilenial butterflies
Biting midges
Lice
Ticks

ASIA
Bat mites
Leeches
Biting midges
Mosquitoes
Vampire moths

AFRICA
Tsetse flies
Mosquitoes
Ticks
Biting midges

AUSTRALIA
March flies
Ticks
Fleas
Lice
Bed bugs

CHAPTER 8

There's a Sucker Born Every Minute

Most bloodsucking creatures are oviparous, which means their young hatch from eggs. But how they develop while inside the egg and their metamorphosis—how they change once they hatch—is different from one creature to another.

LIFE CYCLE OF A MOSQUITO

(1) A female mosquito lays eggs on a body of still water, either one at a time or clumped together in a group of 100 to 200 eggs called a "raft". Mosquitoes will lay their eggs anywhere: in a clogged house gutter, in a bucket, or even in a tiny pool of rainwater collected on a leaf!

(2) After a few days, the eggs hatch and larvae emerge into the water. The larvae will stay near the surface of the water for the next 10 days or so, feeding on all the microscopic **organic material** floating there. They grow so quickly that they will molt four times! During this period, they move through the water using a twitching, wriggling motion that has earned them the nickname of "wrigglers".

(3) Next, they curl up into comma shapes and change into **pupae**, still floating near the surface of the water so they can breathe. They stay like this for about two days.

(4) Then adult mosquitoes emerge from the pupae!

TOP: Mosquito eggs hatch in water.
BOTTOM: Mosquito pupae stay in the water, but close to the surface so they can breathe.

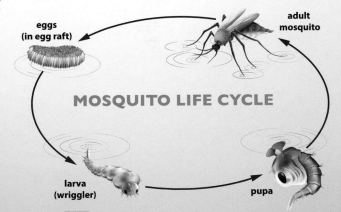

eggs (in egg raft)

adult mosquito

MOSQUITO LIFE CYCLE

larva (wriggler)

pupa

This four-stage process, from egg to larva to pupa to adult, is called "complete metamorphosis". It takes 5 to 40 days in total, depending on the species and the climate.

LIFE CYCLE OF A KISSING BUG

 A female kissing bug lays individual eggs in a nest where there is a readily available food source, such as a packrat den (because packrats stay in their dens for a long time). This usually happens during the months of May through September.

 After anywhere from 10 to 30 days, an egg hatches and a nymph emerges. A nymph is a soft-bodied baby insect, with a head, **thorax**, and abdomen. They have six legs, two eyes, a mouth, and a pair of antennae. Over the next 1 to 2 years, the kissing bug nymph will go through five stages of growing and shedding, surviving on blood meals from the rats as it grows.

③ After the fifth shedding, the nymph turns into an adult with wings. It is time to fly away from the nest and look for its first bloody meal as a grown-up kissing bug!

Because there was no pupal stage, this process from egg to adult is called "incomplete metamorphosis".

There are over 3,500 species of mosquitoes. It is believed that if you added up the total weight of all living mosquitoes and compared it to the total weight of all living humans, they would be the same.

There are many different species of kissing bugs throughout the world—there are 12 in the United States alone!

BLOOD AND GUTS

Vampire moths and their caterpillar larvae, like other insects, have blood that helps move water and other nutrients from their intestines to other parts of their bodies. But because insects don't have red blood cells, their blood (called hemolymph) isn't red! It's clear, or sometimes yellowish or greenish from plant pigments. What happens to this vampire's blood when it goes through metamorphosis? Inside the silky cocoon, the caterpillar pupa shrinks and dissolves into a chunky soup-like mixture. Some organs stay intact but shrink, some grow, and others re-attach themselves in new places. In other words, the vampire moth's blood and guts all mix together. Then when the time is right, a newly formed adult moth goes on the hunt for fresh blood to fill its belly.

The calyptra moth and the madrilenial butterfly both go through metamorphosis, but they do it differently. For one thing, the special packages that they form around their bodies before they go through metamorphosis are different! This table shows how.

Chitin is a hard, translucent substance that is the main component of a chrysalis. Some insects, such as kissing bugs, have chitin exoskeletons.

	Calyptra Moth	Madrilenial Butterfly
What's It Called?	cocoon	chrysalis
What's It Feel Like?	soft	hard
What's It Made Of?	silk	chitin

Vampire Batterfly:

A METAMORPHOSIS GAME

This is a game you can play with a group of friends. It's a little like a cross between volleyball and baseball, but with a metamorphosis twist!

Materials:
- Volleyball
- Four bases

Set Up:
- Divide into two equal teams: outfielders and batters.
- Set out four bases, just like a baseball diamond.

Object of the Game:

Capture the other team's players, while building your own team.

Directions:
- The pitcher serves the ball to the vampire batterfly at home plate.
- The vampire bumps or volleys it.
- Then the vampire flies around the bases, shouting "egg" at first base, "larva" at second base, and "chrysalis" at third base.
- Instead of running home, the vampire must catch another player, all the while calling out "adult bloodsucker." The outfielders must try to tag him with the ball.
- If the vampire catches another player, he takes his victim home to his own team. If he gets tagged first, he is out! The team that captures all of the players from the other team first wins the game.

CHAPTER 9

Parasites from the Past

WEIGHING IN ON FLEAS

Bloodsuckers have been around since the time of the dinosaurs. Recently, scientists found **fossilized** fleas in Inner Mongolia that were 165 million years old. These fleas were up to 20.6 millimetres (0.8 inches) long, about as long as a child's big toe! They were very different from today's fleas. They had flatter bodies, longer antennae and claws, and proboscises that were as long and sharp as needles. The biggest mammals alive at that time were rodents about the size of hamsters, which was way too small to be a host for these fleas. Since modern fleas are known to feed on the blood of birds, **zoologists** and **palaeontologists** believe that these fleas probably either fed on the blood of feathered dinosaurs or used their needle-like proboscises to pierce the tough skin between the scales of larger dinosaurs.

AMBER: AS GOOD AS GOLD?

Amber is a sticky evergreen-tree resin that first oozes out through the tree bark, and then hardens and becomes fossilized over millions of years. It is prized for making beautiful jewellery and ornaments. In prehistoric times, if an insect got caught in the resin before it hardened, that insect would then be preserved as a fossil in amber.

Movies such as *Jurassic Park* make it seem like mosquitoes are commonly found in amber, but these fossils are actually very rare. There is only one mosquito preserved from the Cretaceous period, when dinosaurs lived, and there are only a few dozen more recent samples of mosquitoes in amber. However, there are many other bloodsucking insects whose remains have survived in amber from the Cretaceous period.

Amber is formed when tree resin becomes fossilized.

Paleozoic Era (Permian Period)	Mesozoic Era (Triassic Period)		Mesozoic Era (Jurassic Period)			Mesozoic Era (Cretaceous Period)					Cenozoic Era (Paleogene Period)	
298.9 Million Years Ago	225 Million Years Ago	220 Million Years Ago	176 Million Years Ago	165 Million Years Ago	155 Million Years Ago	135 Million Years Ago	130 Million Years Ago or Earlier	100 Million Years Ago	90 Million Years Ago	65 Million Years Ago	52 Million Years Ago	40 Million Years Ago
Evolution of Beetles	First Dinosaurs	First Crocodilians, Flies, and Mammals (Haramiyids)	First Stegosauruses	First Fleas	First Birds and Ticks	First Sandflies	First Horseflies	First Bees	First Mosquitoes and Black Flies	Extinction of Dinosaurs	First Bats	First Butterflies and Moths

As this table demonstrates, bloodsucking insects and dinosaurs co-existed for millions of years. Therefore, it is possible that dinosaurs and mammals of the past were bugged by these insects as much as people are bugged today.

However, there are many other bloodsucking insects whose remains have survived in amber from the Cretaceous period. Samples exist of biting flies, such as horse-flies and other insects. Dinosaurs and mammals of the past were bugged by these insects as much as people are bugged today.

BLOOD FROM A STONE

Mosquitoes and fleas may have lived with the Tyrannosaurus rex, but cloning dinosaurs from the blood stored in the bellies of fossilized bloodsuckers is impossible for two reasons. First, scientists have determined that DNA, the code for all living things, can only remain preserved for 6.8 million years at the most. But the most recent dinosaur bones are 65 million years old, which means dinosaurs lived way too long ago for there to be any usable DNA left in the fossils of their bloodsucking parasites.

Second, when a bug is preserved in amber, the bacteria and enzymes in the bug's gut continue to digest the bug's soft tissue from the inside out until everything is dissolved but the hard outer shell, or exoskeleton. So most of these preserved bugs are actually hollow! There isn't any blood left inside them at all. Basically, the chances of one day butting heads with the dinosaur king are zero—which is probably a good thing!

DNA, deoxyribonucleic acid, can only stay preserved for a maximum of 6.8 million years.

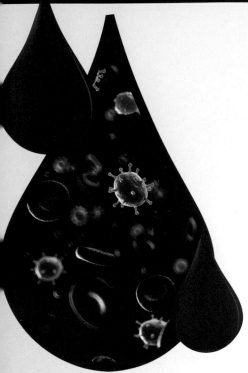

CHAPTER 10

Virus infected blood

Blood, Sweat, and Fears

In addition to being annoying, bloodsucking creatures are considered vectors for diseases, which means that they can carry disease from one host to another. Sometimes, as in the case of Chagas disease, bacteria are present in insect feces. Sometimes, if a host is already infected with a disease and a bloodsucking bug drinks the infected blood, the disease-causing organism multiplies in the bloodsucker's gut. Then when it bites the next host, some of the contents of its gut get injected into that host, and the disease spreads. Because different creatures have different anatomies, the disease often has no effect on the vampire critter. In the case of malaria, for example, the microscopic organism that causes the disease can multiply both in a mosquito's gut and in the red blood cells of humans. Mosquitoes do not feel any effects, but for humans, the destruction of red blood cells can cause serious illness. But sometimes—like in the case of bats carrying rabies, or in the case of fleas carrying bubonic plague—the vampire critter will become infected. In all of these instances, however, the next host to be bitten will become infected with the disease.

Head lice, unlike body lice, do not carry any diseases.

FLEA BITTEN

In medieval times, the average person wasn't very clean. Most families lived crammed into only one or two rooms, and without indoor plumbing, they had no toilets or showers. They used a bucket in the corner of the room as a toilet and were lucky if they managed to bathe every week. What's more, the buckets they used as toilets attracted rats and other creatures to their living quarters. It was common for both people and rats alike to have body lice, fleas, or both.

Body lice and fleas were partly to blame for the spread of diseases like typhus and the **bubonic plague** (also known as the Black Death). Cramped living quarters combined with a thriving population of lice and fleas meant that diseases such as these spread quickly.

Because bacteria (and medicines to fight the bacteria) would not be discovered for hundreds of years, people in medieval Europe relied on folk remedies, or non-medical remedies, to cure or prevent diseases. One thing that medieval people believed would keep the Black Death away was a bouquet of strongly scented flowers, like mint and pennyroyal. People often carried bouquets of these flowers in their pockets to cover the stink from their unwashed bodies. They noticed that people who carried more of these flowers in their pockets were less likely to get sick. The belief that flowers could ward off disease is often put down to silly superstition, but there is some science behind it. Both lice and fleas are repelled by the scents of certain flowers, including mint and pennyroyal, and this could explain why people who carried those flowers were less likely to catch the plague.

Diseases like typhus and the Black Death once wiped out one third of Europe's population. The discovery of bacteria later enabled scientists to develop medicines, called antibiotics (ANT-ee-bye-AWT-icks), which kill the bacteria that cause these deadly diseases.

Certain flowers emit scents that repel some bloodsuckers, like fleas and lice.

TICKED OFF IN NORTHERN CANADA

Ticks are some of the most successful critters that have ever lived. They live everywhere in the world—even in the northern Canadian tundra. Part of their success comes from their exoskeletons (their external shells), which protect them from low temperatures and dehydration. Another part of their success comes from their feeding habits.

These arachnids are good at finding hosts and drinking their blood. They do this with a behaviour called questing: using their front legs to detect the warmth and moisture from a host's breath, a tick stands on its hind legs and waits on a shrub or in the long grass. It only takes one tenth of a second for the tick to climb onto a woodland caribou, reindeer, or similar victim that brushes against the shrub. Once on its host, the tick will puncture its victim with its barbed mouthparts and then drink for several hours until it is engorged.

The tick's feeding makes the caribou itch. The caribou responds by grooming itself with its tongue or by rubbing against a hard surface like a rock.

The bubonic plague's most deadly period was in Europe during the 14th century. But did you know that it is still around? Every year, about seven people in the United States and between 1,000 and 2,000 people worldwide are infected. Fortunately, if it is diagnosed quickly, it can be treated easily with antibiotics.

Ticks live in all sorts of territories around the world.

There are several reasons why ticks can be bothersome for caribou.

 They can carry diseases (e.g., Lyme disease, Rocky Mountain spotted fever).

 The tick may stay on its host for an entire year, raising its family.

③ Depending on how many ticks are living on one host, the caribou can lose a lot of blood over time.

 As the caribou rubs against hard surfaces or over-grooms itself, it may lose its hair, a valuable tool for keeping warm in arctic climates.

⑤ If the caribou is too distracted by ticks, it will spend less time eating, thus becoming thin and malnourished.

THESE WELTS ARE BUGGING ME!

Bed bug bites are painless at first because these bloodsuckers inject an anaesthetic, which numbs the skin. However, in people who react to the bites, itchy red welts may appear by the next morning. If the victim is repeatedly bitten, these welts are often lined up on an area of the body, like the legs or arms.

Unlike mosquitoes, lice, ticks, mites, and fleas, bed bugs are not considered a health hazard because they do not spread diseases. But scratching the itchy welts that they leave behind can lead to secondary skin infections. An infection of this sort, depending on how severe it is, may require medical attention.

FRAUGHT WITH DANGER

In addition to the diseases and the medical threats that various bloodsuckers cause, there are environmental dangers as well.

First, bloodsuckers can be especially dangerous when they are invasive species. Sea lampreys are an example of this environmental threat. When the Welland Canal was completed in 1932, sea lampreys gained access to the Great Lakes. Not only did they drain the blood of new types of

The white-footed mouse is thought to be the main carrier species that spreads ticks infected with Lyme disease from one host, such as caribou, to another.

Sea lampreys pose an environmental threat as an invasive species.

freshwater fish, their large numbers also disrupted the **biodiversity** of the area.

In order to control these growing populations of vampires, people have begun spraying a chemical called a lampricide into the Great Lakes. Lampricide is a pesticide that kills the sea lamprey larvae before they are able to grow into adults and parasitize other creatures. This is dangerous! Though this chemical doesn't cause a threat to most other fish, it does reduce mollusc and amphibian populations. The larvae of amphibians and molluscs are particularly sensitive to lampricide exposure. Spraying this chemical into a drinking water source also doesn't seem like a good idea.

DISEASES CARRIED BY BAD BLOOD

In addition to the Black Death, there are several other diseases that are transmitted by bloodsuckers.

Vampire Creature	Transmitted Disease	Symptoms of the Disease		Prevention or Treatment
Vampire Bat	Rabies	• flu-like symptoms • confusion	• anxiety • hallucinations	Preventable with a vaccine
Kissing Bug	Chagas Disease	Initial symptoms include: • flu-like symptoms • diarrhea • vomiting • redness and swelling at the bite wound After recovery and decades of good health: • heart disease • organ failure • problems with the stomach and intestines		Treatable in early stages through prescription medication
Deer Tick	Lyme Disease	• flu-like symptoms • stiff neck • swelling of the lining • arthritis around the brain • lack of control of facial muscles • red, spreading, "bull's-eye" rash		Treatable in early stages with antibiotics
Mosquito	Malaria	• high fever • shaking • chills • flu-like illness		Preventable and treatable with anti-malarial medication
	West Nile Virus	In Most Cases: • flu-like symptoms In Rare Cases: • stiff neck • confusion • severe headache • sensitivity to light		No treatment is needed for mild cases. Rare severe cases must be cared for in the hospital.
Fleas	Bubonic Plague (Black Death)	• swollen lymph nodes • fever • muscle cramps • seizures • blackening and infection of the fingers, toes, lips, and nose		Treatable in early stages with antibiotics

CHAPTER 11

Vampires: Keeping Us Safe and Sound

The effects of vampire critters on humans aren't all bad: they offer hidden benefits, too. Doctors and scientists have made several medical and technological breakthroughs thanks to what we have learned by studying bloodsuckers and how they live.

OPENING THE BLOOD GATES

Our ancestors believed that any condition that reddened skin tones, such as a fever or an inflammation, could be cured using leeching. Originating in Greece and India, leeching referred to a medical procedure where leeches were placed on patients' skin and allowed to feed on their blood. It was believed that using leeches in this way could balance patients' humours and thus improve their overall health. Back then, humours were known as blood, phlegm, yellow bile, and black bile—four fluids then believed to affect a person's mood and well-being. This continued throughout history right into the late 19th century, when doctors would practise bloodletting by inserting a metal tube into a patient's arm and allowing blood to flow out into a bowl. To some extent, these ancient civilizations were right—for example, people with high blood pressure experienced an improvement in symptoms. However, the beliefs about balancing humours have since been proven incorrect by medical science. And while draining blood does make someone's skin tone

Doctors use sphygmomanometers (SFIG-mow-muh-NAH-muh-turz) to measure blood pressure, which is the pressure exerted by the blood on the inner walls of the blood vessels as it is pumped throughout the body.

paler, it doesn't do anything to treat an infection. In fact, the reduced number of white blood cells makes it even harder to fight an infection! We now know that bloodletting is a dangerous practice.

Today, leeches are used in **microsurgeries** to remove infected blood from the body. Since untreated infections can spread, and in extreme cases can lead to the loss of an arm or a leg, leeches can save a limb! They can also remove pooled blood from a wound, which prevents blood clots from forming as the wound heals. This reduces the risk of a stroke occurring later. Leeches can drink up to five times their own body weight and they are cheap and efficient, so they offer a natural alternative to post-surgery antibiotics and blood-thinning medications.

FLEA FOR YOUR LIFE

Fleas are jumping marvels. Inspired by these miraculous high jumpers, electrical engineers have started creating miniature flea robots. These tiny robots are equipped with chemical sensors for the purpose of identifying whether an area is a safe place for people to be.

When dropped from a plane, these robots may not land exactly where they are supposed to. However, because these robots are built just like fleas and are made to be excellent jumpers, they can be programmed to hop over uneven ground to the target location. Then they can safely relay information back to militaries and governments about unsafe spaces. They can sense radiation, land mines, and explosives. These robots can also sense through walls, determining if dangerous materials are inside buildings. They let organizations know in advance whether it is safe to send people to that area.

Fleas are incredible jumpers. Using their multi-jointed hind legs, they can jump 100 to 150 times their own height. That's like a child jumping to the top of the Eiffel Tower!

KISSING SYRINGES GOODBYE

Zoos in England might be saying goodbye to medical **syringes** in the near future, thanks to some research that has been done with kissing bugs.

Taking blood samples from large zoo mammals can be both stressful for the animals and dangerous for the zookeepers or veterinarians. Blood samples need to be taken occasionally in order to ensure the mammals are healthy. Rather than using bulky constraints and fearsome syringes, why not let a bloodsucker do the job?

When a hungry kissing bug is released into an animal enclosure at meal time, it will find its host and begin feeding within 10 to 30 minutes. No pain is caused to the mammal because the kissing bug injects a pain-reducing enzyme as it pierces its victim's skin and begins drawing blood. Once adequate blood samples are drawn, the insect is collected and destroyed. Meanwhile, the mammal's blood is now available to be studied by the zoo's medical staff.

BATTLING HEART ATTACKS

Scientists have managed to isolate the anticoagulant enzyme in vampire bats' saliva. They named it "Draculin", after Dracula, the mythical creature that gives vampire bats their name. After studying the structure of this enzyme, and after studying its behaviour when combined with other substances found in blood, scientists believe that it can be used to develop a medication that will bust up blood clots in humans. This will help prevent heart attacks and strokes.

CHAPTER 12

Suck It Up: We Need Those Bloodsuckers!

MARVELLOUS MOSQUITOES

As you know, mosquitoes can be real pests. Females keep you awake, buzz in your ear, and suck your blood through their straw-like proboscises. Worse, they carry diseases such as malaria, yellow fever, Japanese encephalitis, and West Nile virus. Some scientists are currently discussing ways to eliminate the species of mosquito that most commonly transmits diseases to humans. However, other scientists argue that eradicating any species—even this pesky mosquito species—can have significant, and perhaps negative, environmental effects.

Though annoying, lots of species depend on mosquitoes for their survival. For example, many fish feed on mosquito larvae. Spiders, birds, lizards, and frogs also eat mosquitoes. Although bats mainly eat moths, they have been known to chow down on these nocturnal pests, too. According to **entomologist** Richard Merritt, "Mosquitoes are delectable things to eat and they're easy to catch." Mosquitoes also help keep our ponds clean because, as larvae, they feed on decaying leaves, organic debris, and microorganisms.

So next time you eat a fish dinner, see the bottom of a pond, or have a dragonfly land on your shoulder, you can thank a mosquito—it probably played a small part in what you are experiencing at some point. In these ways, mosquitoes are part of our ecosystem and benefit humans.

TOP: Mosquitoes, though pesky and sometimes dangerous, play a vital role in our ecosystem.

BOTTOM: Whether it's cleaning up our ponds or being a tasty snack for frogs, mosquitoes contribute to our environment.

BLOOD ON THE BATTLEFIELD

Guano is a fancy word for bat poop. Bat guano is very nutritious for plants—it's an excellent fertilizer. Using bat guano to fertilize fields is beneficial to farmers. When vampire bats poop and pee in a field after feeding, the field is fertilized automatically. Additionally, farmers in regions where bats live can harvest bat guano from the bats' caves and either use it on their own fields, or sell it to other farmers, or both.

STUCK IN A WEB

A food web is a map of the connections between all living things: who eats what, and who is eaten by whom. It is tempting to think of these things as straight lines, like chains, from the smallest things up to the biggest things. But most creatures eat more than one thing, and most creatures are eaten by more than one predator. So instead of a food chain, we suggest a food web. All living things fit into food webs, especially bloodsuckers! Here is one small piece of the food web that includes bloodsuckers:

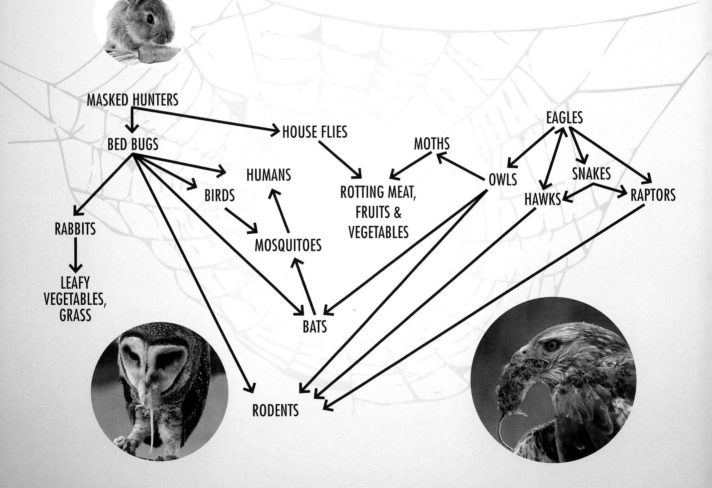

Food webs are important because they show that all living things depend on all other living things for survival—they are interdependent. The disappearance of one species from a food web can have a lasting impact on all the other species in the web.

CHAPTER 13

Leave My Blood Alone!

STOP BUGGING ME!

Bloodsuckers are everywhere. But are they dangerous? Most bites are usually harmless, even when they are really itchy. But sometimes mosquito bites or bites from other bloodsucking critters can spread diseases, like Lyme disease, the bubonic plague, West Nile virus, and malaria. So, it's important to avoid them whenever we can. Fortunately, there are lots of easy things you can do to help yourself and others avoid these parasites.

WHAT YOU CAN DO FOR YOURSELF AND YOUR FAMILY:

Clothing

- Ticks and mosquitoes like to hide in dark, shaded areas, away from the hot sun. Avoid these critters by wearing long-sleeved, light coloured shirts and pants outside. It's also a good idea to tuck your pants into your socks.
- Make sure you check your hair and body for ticks whenever you come in from a wooded area.
- Change your clothes regularly and bathe regularly to avoid body lice.
- Keep your hat and hairbrush to yourself! Sharing those items can spread head lice.

Inside the House

- Fluff your blankets every morning in the winter, and fold them neatly at the foot of your bed to minimize the breeding ground for bed bugs.
- Vacuum your mattress once a week to prevent bed bugs from establishing a home there.
- Do not pick up used upholstered furniture or used mattresses.
- Wash your sheets and pillowcases in hot water once a week.
- Check hotel mattresses for bed bugs.
- Wash all of your clothes when you return home from a vacation.
- Cut down on clutter—cluttered areas are attractive to rodents that could bring mites and fleas into your home.

Head lice can be treated with a special shampoo and comb, but you can avoid getting head lice by tying your hair back and not sharing hairbrushes or hats.

Outside

* Wear a natural insect repellent like the one in the section below when you go outside.
* Keep a fan on the patio or porch in the hot summer months, and turn it on whenever people sit outside. The breeze from the fan will blow the carbon dioxide away, and also make it harder for mosquitoes to reach you.
* Stay away from squirrels and other wild animals! They may look cute, but the fleas they carry won't hesitate to bite you if they get the chance.
* Ask your parents to help you check that there are no cracks or holes on the outside of your house that small rodents could use to enter, bringing their bloodsucking parasites with them.
* Ask your vet about prescribing flea treatments or flea collars for your outdoor pets.

There are some smells that bloodsucking pests can't stand. You can use these scents to make your own all-natural bug repellent!

BUG OFF!

Some people believe that mosquitoes, lice, ticks, and fleas love the smell of carbon dioxide, which all mammals exhale as we breathe. To a bloodsucking insect, carbon dioxide means dinner is close by! But there are some scents that these puny pests will avoid at all costs. For example, studies have shown that mosquitoes don't like the smell of eucalyptus oil or cinnamon oil, and fleas stay away from orange oil. Here is a simple recipe you can follow to create an effective all-natural bug repellent.

You will need:
* apple cider vinegar or a mild-smelling vegetable oil, like canola or sunflower oil
* eucalyptus essential oil
* cinnamon essential oil
* orange essential oil
* spray bottle
* funnel
* measuring cups

 Using the funnel, pour 1/2 cup of apple cider vinegar or four tablespoons of vegetable oil into the empty spray bottle.

Carefully add 20 drops of eucalyptus oil, 16 drops of orange oil, and 14 drops of cinnamon oil to the apple cider vinegar or oil in the spray bottle. (Get an adult to help you if you need to.)

 Twist the top on tightly and shake the mixture well.

Whenever you want to go outside, shake the mixture and spray it onto your arms, legs, and any other exposed skin, but *not* your face! To apply it to your face, spray a little onto your fingertips and rub it onto your cheeks and neck. If your parents give you permission, you can even safely spray it onto your clothes! Have fun, and remember to re-spray every two hours to keep the bugs at bay.

THE CLOCK IS TICKING

Finding a bloodsucking bug on your body can be pretty gross. Your first instinct might be to swat it off. But if the bug is a tick with its head burrowed into your skin, swatting it off could just get rid of the tick's body—and leave its head stuck inside you! This can lead to a nasty infection. On the other hand, if you wait for it to finish feeding and walk away, you could end up waiting for hours! Of course, avoiding ticks is the best idea, but if you get stuck with a tick on you, there are safer ways for an adult to help you get rid of it. Here is a list of DOs and DON'Ts:

DON'T	DO
Don't try to pull it off with your bare fingers. You might accidentally squeeze infected blood back into your body, get infected blood on your fingers, or give the tick another chance to bite you on the hand.	Protect hands by wearing rubber gloves or covering fingers with tissue paper.
Don't flick it off. This can leave the tick's head stuck inside your skin, and cause an infection around the wound.	Grasp the tick's head with fine-tipped tweezers. Get as close to its mouthparts as possible.
Don't try to squeeze or twist it out. It will probably just get annoyed and burrow even deeper into your skin. Twisting can break the head off and leave it stuck inside you.	Pull the tick straight out, away from your body, without twisting.
Don't smother the tick with petroleum jelly or soap. This could make the tick release infected fluid back into your body.	Pull slowly and gently.
Don't try to burn it out with a match. You are more likely to burn yourself!	Be patient, and sit still! Slow, gentle pulling with tweezers will make the tick let go eventually.

The species of mosquito that spreads dengue fever doesn't travel far. Adults remain within 200 metres (656 feet) of their hatching sites.

To prevent the spread of dengue fever, scientists have discovered a way to breed male mosquitoes that are unable to reproduce. When the scientists release them, these males mate with the female mosquitoes and ensure that no offspring are produced. This means there are fewer mosquitoes around to spread dengue fever. They hope to use the same strategy to battle malaria.

PLANET-WIDE PEST CONTROL

In some parts of the world, such as Sub-Saharan Africa and South Asia, mosquitoes spread malaria. If you plan to travel to an area where malaria is common, one easy way to protect yourself from becoming infected is to make sure that there is a mosquito net covering your sleeping area. Your parents can also ask your doctor for anti-malarial medication that you can take for several days in advance of your trip. One day, doctors hope to be able to offer anti-malarial vaccines.

DON'T BE A SUCKER!

Most people think about vampire creatures and turn up their noses. The thought of lice, fleas, and bed bugs makes many people squeamish. And why wouldn't they? Bloodsuckers are specially designed to drink blood—sometimes your blood. They are often small and sometimes deadly.

Vampire creatures can be a nuisance, but they can also be helpful. They are necessary for our ecosystems and they help to diversify our world.

Educating ourselves about vampire creatures can be our best defence against bites and diseases, and might be the best way to create a world that is better able to sustain the diverse creatures that live here. Indeed, education can also make us more knowledgeable, enable us to interpret the world around us, offer helpful strategies for living, and help us hold ourselves accountable for our actions. It is estimated that there are more than 500 trillion bloodsuckers living on this planet. They are not going away. We can be suckers and ignore them, or we can make a difference.

Index

Glossary

ANTICOAGULANT a substance that makes blood runnier, increasing blood flow and preventing blood from clotting

BIODIVERSITY the existence of a wide variety of plant and animal species in their natural environments

BIOLOGIST a scientist who specializes in the study of living organisms, including animals and plants

BLOOD PRESSURE the pressure exerted by the blood on the inner walls of the blood vessels as it is pumped throughout the body; high blood pressure is an indication that the heart is working harder to pump blood throughout the body

BUBONIC PLAGUE a serious, sometimes fatal bacterial infection; primary symptoms are fever, weakness, and swollen lymph nodes in the groin and armpits

CARBON DIOXIDE a gas, sometimes written as CO_2, that forms part of Earth's atmosphere; it is exhaled as a waste product when we breathe; it is essential for plants to survive; in high levels, it can form a blanket in the upper atmosphere that traps heat from the sun

ENTOMOLOGIST a person who specialises in the study of insects

ENZYME an organic substance that breaks down matter by causing a chemical transformation

FOSSILIZED the state in which the tissues of a dead organism have been replaced over time by dissolved minerals which harden into rock

GILL SLITS openings on the sides of an aquatic animal that allow oxygen-rich water to flow into the animal and over its gills

HABITAT a place where a creature lives

HORMONES chemicals that are produced and excreted by living creatures; they change depending on mood and gender

HOST a plant or animal which provides a food source and/or habitat for a parasite

IMMUNE SYSTEM the system of white blood cells and antibodies by which a living organism fights disease

IRON one of the basic elements of the universe, this metal makes it possible for red blood cells to transport oxygen, and is therefore essential for survival

LABELLA the sponge-like lobe at the tip of a fly's proboscis

LARVA the immature, wingless, feeding stage of an insect that undergoes complete metamorphosis; sometimes referred to as a grub or caterpillar

MAMMAL a creature which gives birth to live young, breathes air, and suckles its young

MICROSURGERY any surgical procedure performed using magnification to aid the surgeon, with small, specialized instruments

ORGANIC MATERIAL carbon-based tissues of creatures and plants

PALAEONTOLOGIST a person who specializes in the study of past life forms by examining their fossilized remains

PARASITE a creature that lives off of other creatures, without eating them, in order to survive

PROBOSCIS the straw-like mouthparts of certain bloodsucking creatures, used for piercing and/or sucking

PUPA the usually non-feeding, immobile transformation stage of an insect from larva to adult

SYRINGE a needle and hollow plastic, glass, or rubber cylinder with a plunger; used for either injecting or collecting blood or other fluids

THORAX the part of an insect's body that is between the head and abdomen and to which the legs and wings are attached

VERTEBRATE any living creature that has a spinal column

ZOOLOGIST a scientist who specializes in studying animals

Further Reading

BOOKS

Muraski, D. & Honovich, N. *Ultimate Bugopedia: The Most Complete Bug Reference Ever.* National Geographic Children's Books, 2013.

Somervil, B. *Vampire Bats: Hunting for Blood.* Powerkids Press, 2007.

VIDEOS

Nature's Vampires. http://www.youtube.com/watch?v=5pysO5JyDDk

WEBPAGES

"American Academy of Dermatology" http://www.aad.org/dermatology-a-to-z/diseases-and-treatments/e---h/head-lice.

"The Bioluminescence Web Page." http://www.lifesci.ucsb.edu/~biolum/.

"Great Lakes Fishery Commission." http://www.glfc.org/sealamp/.

"Leeches Cure." http://video/places/regions-places/asia-travel/india_leechescure/.

"Mayo Clinic." http://www.mayoclinic.org.

Naish, Darren, "Vampire Finches and the Path to Parasitism," Tetrapod Zoology, 2007, http://scienceblogs.com/tetrapodzoology/2007/02/01/vampire-finches-and-the-path-t/.

Nordic Recipe Archive, Meat Dishes, "Blood Pancakes", 1997-2014, http://www.dlc.fi/~marian1/gourmet/7_20.htm.

Ross, Andrew interviewing Jeremy Austin, "The Search for DNA in Amber," Natural History Museum, UK, http://www.nhm.ac.uk/resources-rx/files/12feat_dna_in_amber-3007.pdf.

"Top 10 Bloodsuckers." http://www.animalplanet.com/tv-shows/animal-planet-presents/videos/top-10-bloodsuckers-madrilenial-butterfly.htm.

"Vampire Moths Discovered: Evolution at Work." http://nationalgeographic.com/video/news/animals-news/vampire-moth-vin/.

Bibliography

The full list of works cited can be found on our website at www.fitzhenry.ca/biteintobloodsuckers/

Image Credits